SOAR!

Empowering Tools for the Classroom & Beyond

Jennifer L. Coon

DEDICATION

In memory of my grandma, Fae, a model teacher who showed me how to love unconditionally and guide without force or control.

CONTENTS

Contents

ACKNOWLEDGMENTS

I would like to acknowledge a fellow right-brained warrior, Kirk A. Duncan, president of 3 Key Elements. Because he battled his own negative messages and was determined to share with others what he had learned, I was able to learn about the tools in this book. I too am determined to share what I have learned as I have seen transformation in my students, their parents, my fellow teachers, and in myself. I hope that many teachers transform their classrooms as well, thereby helping millions of children identify and achieve their purpose.

Thanks, Kirk!

And

Special thanks to my editing team:
Marsha Coon, Fawn Duncan, and Jean Duncan
I love your dominant left brains!

INTRODUCTION

This book would not be a reality if it had not been for the amazing things I have learned, and the work I have put into taking a hard look at myself. It can be so easy to look at others and find fault and things that need improvement. But, how willing are we to do that to ourselves? A few years ago I knew I wasn't happy with myself, but I wasn't sure how I could begin to change things. I didn't feel like I needed help from a counselor or therapist, but deep down I knew there was more for me to do and I was on a one way street to nowhere. In essence, I was in survival mode.

When I started learning more and more about myself and the way I "tick", I began to have a better understanding of humanity in general and the common threads that tie us together. The knowledge I gained was priceless. I was finally soaring!

Then, one day, I decided to use the knowledge I had gained to help my students break free from survival mode. What happened was amazing! I knew that if both my second graders and I could experience transformation, anyone could! It then became my mission to share what I had learned, but deep inside I felt the need to remain a teacher. How could I spread my message and remain in the classroom? I did my best, training and mentoring evenings and weekends, but it still did not feel like enough. Then, just a few short weeks ago, while feeding my chickens, I felt inspired to write this book.

At first I felt those nauseating butterflies creep in, but then I was propelled forward! I know this message is something I must share with as many people as possible. It is my hope you will gain much from what is in this book, and that you will use it to help others, also.

The tools in the book can be used in any order. I would encourage you to read through them and mark up the book. It is a tool and resource unto itself, not a fiction novel. Start with one tool that strikes a chord with you. After you use it yourself, you will be an expert and ready to share with others. Then continue on... Have a wonderful journey!

Here's to SOARING!

JEN

1
MY FOUNDATION

Okay. So, before you read any further, I must warn you that I am a human being. I make mistakes. It is from those mistakes I have become the "AMAZING" person I am today. In this book you will undoubtedly find errors, those evidences that I am indeed human. If you cannot handle humanness, go ahead and close this book now and pass it on to someone who can.

Still reading? Great! I am so glad you decided to stay and play! To quote one of my favorite teachers, Ms. Frizzle of the Magic School Bus, "Take chances, make mistakes, and get messy!" Before I ever heard her declare those words to her students, I lived by those words. My father often warned me that I learned things the hard way. In actuality, I was just following my heart and it sometimes ended up looking a bit messy.

But, boy howdy, I sure have made mistakes and gotten messy... especially during my own formative education days. To sum it all up, let me take you back to the night of my high school graduation…

I pulled up to the Don Haskins Center in my 1980 Delta 88 Oldsmobile. The butterflies in my stomach felt as though they were battling to find their way out. I kept thinking to myself, "*Surely they would have told me if I hadn't qualified to graduate.*" I knew it was going to be close. I had to pass the Algebra II class or else… Getting tutoring from my former middle school math teacher, I had battled my way through the semester. From what I could tell, graduating hinged on that final test.

Walking inside, I felt the excitement in the air, but it was not shared by me. I had no idea what my final grades were. I nearly choked on one of those butterflies. Everything seemed so unreal. Fear consumed my consciousness.

Surely they would have told me.

I found my place amongst the 700+ other graduates. We marched in, and the ceremony began. I cannot remember who spoke, who our valedictorian was, or who was even there from my family. I just remember the worry that consumed me.

Surely they would have told me.

Finally, the moment of truth arrived, the row I was sitting in filed to the aisle. I saw my algebra teacher sitting there in her fancy master's robe. Desperately, I tried to meet her gaze.

Please tell me if I didn't pass your class. Oh, wait, do you even know my name?

Insecure and alone amongst thousands of people, I suddenly found myself at the front of the line. Ahhh, I was freaking out! I saw myself on the Jumbo-trons. I was next!

Surely they would have told me.

Then, the unthinkable happened. They didn't call my name! They called the guy behind me! I glanced up to the Jumbo-trons and witnessed the look of terror on my face. Now those who know me, and don't even have to know me well, will verify how the expressions on my face can be read like a book. I was frantic! The butterflies were now gagging me and robbing me of oxygen. *Okay... pull yourself together, Jen. Now think... what would be the best way to get out of here without too many people noticing?* Just as I was about to run for my life, I glanced up to the stage and locked eyes with one of the counselors. She raised her hand in a staying motion as if to say, *Just wait.* Half of me trusted and locked my feet to the ground. The other half questioned her. *Do you even know me? Do you even know my name? How do you know they have a diploma up there for me?* After all, they had just called the guy behind me for goodness sake!

The trust paid off. They called me next after what seemed like an eternity. I shook hands, received my diploma, and dropped dead butterflies with each step as I returned to my seat. I cannot remember the rest of the ceremony. I was just glad I had graduated with my 2.?? G.P.A.

So, some of you may be wondering by now what qualifications I have to teach you about essential classroom elements? I bring you a different type of perspective from most individuals who write educational books. What? That's correct! Many people who have my brain dominance succumb to the thought that they are not smart. For me, logic and facts are hard to absorb, but, boy howdy, I am creative! I would bet that many of the books that fill our bookshelves pertaining to education have been written by dominant left-brained people. Most left-brainers do well in school! Yay for all you left-brained people! But, our classrooms do not just have left-brained dominant people. There are also right-brained dominant people like me. People in education have taken notice of this. In the last decade, there has been an increase of books and trainings available about differentiation. Teachers have better learned how to embrace diverse learning styles.

With what I have learned over the last 30+ years as a fellow human, from my own life experiences and from others, along with what I have discovered as a teacher for 10 years, I now know some essential foundational elements. I use these elements in my classroom and have taught others to use them in their classrooms. The results have been amazing! I know this is something I need to share with as many people, especially teachers, as I can. It is not complicated. It does not require expensive resources. And on the bonus side, this book is written by someone who is self-diagnosed as having A.D.D. and does not enjoy reading (but please don't tell my students that). Therefore, this information will be direct and to the point! You will be able to implement this in no time! It just requires an understanding and a willingness to try. Are you ready to take your classroom to the next level? Then keep reading!

2
VARIETY IS THE GARDEN OF LIFE

Thank goodness theories in education support the idea that people learn in different ways. People also are believed to have a dominant side of the brain they prefer to use, much like a dominant hand. Which side of the brain is your dominant side? There are fun little quizzes you may take online as a beginning step to find out. Below, I have included a brief summary of what the different hemispheres of the brain are responsible for:

Left hemisphere	Right hemisphere
Logic	Creativity
Sequence	Intuition
Language: grammar/vocab.	Language: tone
Direct fact retrieval	Visualizing the "big picture"

Something interesting to note is that not all research regarding brain hemispheres agrees with each other. The descriptions I have listed previously are the common threads. The hemispheres of the brain do not completely operate independently. They are interconnected. Even though most people prefer to "play" on one side of the brain versus the other, it is important to develop the other side as well.

I do not claim to be an expert in this area, but based on what I have observed during my ten years of teaching, one thing I know for certain is that we are all diverse learners and we all have different strengths and weaknesses. I love the variety of humans on this planet. It reminds me of pictures of fabulous English gardens. Different colors, textures, and heights are all working together to make something beautiful. It can be challenging to meet the various needs of individual students, but with the same love and care gardeners show for their gardens, classrooms can bloom and flourish, too.

So, how do we get that show-stopping garden? It all starts with a good foundation. I, and teachers I have shared this information with, have found that by using the skills and tools presented in this book, a rich foundation is laid. With daily cultivating and enrichment, the basis for a productive classroom will be in place. After the foundation is prepared, any skills you desire or are required to teach will have a fertile location to take root within your students. Once those skills have taken root, it is absolutely essential to continuously tend to the foundation in order for your students to bloom and flourish.

The foundation consists of five essential tools:
- A declaration or affirmation
- Knowing who one is and who one wants to become
- Goals to accomplish
- Journaling
- Music

Now, I must emphasize the importance of good classroom management techniques in addition to this foundation. I will not be detailing classroom management in this book, but without consistency, routines, and expectations for behavior, the above foundation will not be sufficient. I view good classroom management as equivalent to the air and sunlight plants need to thrive.

So, imagine with me. Come on... Don't be shy... For you people who like to play in right-brained land, this is your moment to shine. For my left-brained fans, humor me for a bit. I promise it will not hurt and as a reward for playing in the land of imagination with me, I will feed your brain with some awesome logic and details later. Okay? Anyway, we were getting ready to imagine...

Your students walk into the classroom each morning with a sense of purpose. They know why they are there. They understand how what you are teaching them relates to their future. They know how to battle those negative feelings they brought in with them without involving you in the process. They are productive and happy. Discipline problems are a thing of the past.

Okay, thanks for playing! Now are you ready for the kicker? This is not a make-believe classroom. This is my classroom and the classrooms of those teachers who *apply* the skills and tools I have shared with them. Would you like to have the same results? Yes? Put on your seat-belt then. I'm about to push the big, red button for the rocket boosters… Here we go! 3, 2, 1, BLAST OFF! WHEEEEEEEEEEEEEEE!

3
BREAKING THE ATTACHMENT TO NEGATIVITY:
AFFIRMATIONS/ DECLARATIONS

So y'all, there is a reality out there that most seem to not take much notice of. There are some not so nice messages that play in our minds about ourselves. Need a reminder? How about: *You cannot do it. You are not smart. You don't belong.* Ring a bell? No? Perhaps it is because you now own those messages and believe them to be fact. When that happens the *you* is replaced with an *I*. Check these out now: *I cannot do it. I am not smart. I don't belong.*

Have you ever wondered where those messages come from and how long you have been listening to them? What are the negative messages that go through your mind? Are the ones I wrote above any of your frequent flyers?

Go on and make a list of your top ten negative statements that you seem to "hear" most about yourself. I'll give you some space to do this here just in case you are sitting on a beach somewhere reading this fabulous book and have no paper. Well, that could mean you have no pen either... hum... well, in that case perhaps the nice little elderly lady doing the crossword puzzle a few chairs down can loan you her pen in exchange for help with number 2, across.

The Top Ten Yucky Negative Messages That Go Through My Head:

_____

_____

_____

_____

_____

_____

_____

_____

_____

_____

Okay, now for the really sad part? One day, I asked my second graders to do this same thing. Would you like to know what they said? See if any of these statements sound familiar. Now remember, these came from seven and eight year olds.

1. You are not good enough.
2. People think I don't care.
3. You don't know it.
4. Nobody likes me.
5. I am ugly.
6. People are mad at me.
7. The whole world is against me.
8. I am all alone.
9. Nobody understands me.
10. I am not smart.
11. This is too hard.
12. Teachers don't care about me.
13. You are not as good.

We made this list as a whole class. It took everything I had to maintain my composure. Especially when one student raised his hand and gave me number seven "The whole world is against me." Seven years old and already feeling so isolated!

So what had influenced me to do this activity in the first place? I will need to share a bit of personal information with you. Well, I guess that is okay, right? After all, you know that my high school G.P.A. was a 2.??

Back in October of 2010, someone was indirectly talking about something that struck a chord deep down inside me. As a result, a yucky, negative feeling came over me. It was so strong that I actually had thoughts of ending it all. Luckily those thoughts were temporary, thanks to aid from my higher power, but it had been enough to scare me.

A few months later, a close friend of mine called me up and asked if I would be willing to help her practice to become a mentor. She told me that for each session we would talk over the phone once a week. I enjoyed our discussions and learned to remove the blinders and began to see myself for who I am. During one of our sessions, I will never forget the clarity that my mentor helped me to see. She helped me to discover how one of my biggest, yuckiest, negative messages is *I DON'T BELONG*. That took me back to that dark evening in October. That was the message, but it was buried so deep inside my mind that I felt the message and believed it to be fact. Where did it come from? Did the source really matter? Bottom line was that I didn't want it anymore! That was when I learned of this skill. The trick with these negative messages is first to catch and identify them. Next, comes the part where we find the "record button" deep within ourselves to create a new, positive reality. This is where the use of a declaration or affirmation comes in.

Once the offending message has been identified, the key is to write the opposite down. For maximum impact, it is best to write an additional supportive message that correlates with the original negative message. For example, my big offender was: *I don't belong*. So I wrote down the opposite with additional dose of positive: *I am a valuable person on our planet and I have much to share.*

After writing down those yucky, negative messages that go through my students' minds during school, we worked on writing the opposite of each to make our class declaration. Some of the negative messages were similar so we did not do all of them and, to keep it simple for my second graders, we did not add the additional supportive message like I did in the previous paragraph.

Here is what we ended up with and we called it, The Truth:

The Truth

I am good enough.
I care about people.
I know things.
People like me.
I am pretty/ handsome.
I am not alone.
People understand me.
I am smart.
When it is hard, I can figure it out!
Teachers care about me.
I am good.

After we concluded, we read our new class declaration together. The energy shift in the classroom was tangible. I could literally feel the dark cloak that had been looming over our classroom be blown away. The students took notice, as evident in the large smiles that adorned their faces.

Now it's your turn to turn those yucky thoughts around. Please use this space to record your declaration about who you are.

_____

_____

_____

_____

_____

_____

_____

_____

_____

_____

_____

_____

_____

_____

_____

    I have my own declarations I read to help create a
positive reality. I read them anytime I need a reminder,
but especially at the beginning and end of each day. My
truths change as needed and I have become skilled at
identifying and reversing new yucky thoughts that like
to pop up.

    My students also received their own copy of The
Truth and read it out loud each morning as a part of
their a.m. schedule when they came to school each day.
I asked them what they felt when saying the truth.
Here are some of their responses:

"When I say the truth it makes me feel AWESOME inside! Because it gets the yuckies out of me."

(This child was looking forward to creating her own truth after we returned from winter break. She also included an illustration of herself with The Truth in in her hand.)

"It helps me learn and think! It makes me feel proud and awesome!"

(At the beginning of the school year, I was concerned that I may need to refer this student for testing for special education services. She would become easily frustrated and shut down. Her academic performance shot up to a proficient level and I could no longer see the need for a referral.)

"I feel very happy when I do the truth because I take the yuckies away!"

(I love the power in the word "I" in this statement.)

"The truth makes me feel happy because it's a good thing to say when you feel sad."

"The truth makes me feel great, awesome, and spectacular because the feeling of saying it makes me feel that way."

(I will never forget this student. When we were writing down the negative statements in August, this was the one who told me he felt like the whole world was against him. The emotion in his voice when he shared this was profound. I later found out from his mother that he had been kicked out of his previous school because they said they could not meet his unique needs. He would say The Truth each day with so much feeling that I could sense an energy shift in the classroom. He became one of my top performing students and enjoyed teaching the class a science lesson each Friday.)

"I feel awesome because I do the truth every morning and the yuckies run away."

(I loooove this! I can so imagine that!)

"I feel happy because I practiced my goals and truth. I get happier when I say the truth and goals and *tell my brain what I want.*"

"It makes me happy because it makes me feel better heart and brain and that is the end."

"I feel magic!"

(This student rarely smiled since coming to our school in Kindergarten. He would even have a scowl. By the end of the year, he would share his most beautiful smile all the time and raise his hand to participate in class.)

The use of affirmations and declarations are not new concepts to the planet, but I had never before thought of using them in my classroom and I am so glad I tried it! When the voices of many come together to read positive messages, the result is an increase of positive energy that encompasses the room. Now is this something I can quantify? No. But for those of you who need proof, try it for yourself. Try it with your class! Take note of how things feel afterward. Does this "work" for upper grades? You bet! I have taught this strategy to middle and high school teachers and have received positive feedback.

Negative statements are bombarding students, parents, and teachers all the time! I have shared with you how reversing those negative messages can assist humans in finding the record button deep in the subconscious. Break those attachments with negativity and record a new, positive message to enter the mind! Read those positive statements with conviction and power and do it often!

Tool in a nutshell:
Declarations/ Affirmations
Why? What is the purpose? Declarations aid in breaking the cycle of negativity by reversing the negative statements we "hear" into positive statements.

- Write down the negative message(s) that you "hear" about *yourself*.
- Address one message at a time.
    - Write the opposite of that message.
    - Write an additional positive message that complements the new opposite message you just created.
    - Continue until all the offending negative messages have been addressed.
- Read your new declaration with power and conviction. (The first time I did, I went to the top of the mountain and screamed it. Boy howdy, was that memorable!)
- Put it in a place you will visit often.
- Read it whenever you need a boost.

- No matter what, at the minimum read it in the morning to start your day on a positive track.
- Declarations are not meant to be stagnant. Be aware of your thoughts and feelings. If new, negative messages crash your party, create or change your declaration by following the steps above.

Variations: **Declarations/ Affirmations**

- The same process above can be done with a group of people to create a group declaration.
- Students should be encouraged to create their own after they are guided through the process as a group.

Let's do some reflecting now. Use the t-chart below to write down how using affirmations/ declarations can improve your life and how you can use them to improve another's life.

Your Life	Another's Life

4
WHO ARE YOU?
WHAT IS YOUR PURPOSE?:
WHO I AM

We all remember those "what I want to be when I grow up" activities. Some of us even do them in our classrooms. They usually involve choosing a profession, some crayons, glue, and paper. Those projects may even find a special place on the bulletin board for a while and then make their way home.

What would you think if I told you that such a project was indeed a powerful resource? A way to instill purpose and illustrate one's strengths? Truth is, there are countless numbers of people walking around without a clue as to who they are and what their purpose is. They are merely going through the motions and allowing life to happen to them. How do I know this? Well, in addition to being a teacher, I am also a mentor. After working with a mentor myself, I saw the value of it. I have learned skills needed to help others the way my own mentor helped me, and I am learning more and more with each passing day.

I now have a wonderful team of individuals who are helping me train and mentor teachers so they too may SOAR!   Our   organization   is   called   Classroom Elements.

The mission of Classroom Elements is to empower others to:

See with new eyes.

Open their hearts.

And

Rise to their potential.

As I have mentored a variety of people, including teachers, educational assistants, administrators, parents, and students, I have found that many do not have a clear purpose or mission themselves. It is interesting to observe how people who do not know who they are and what their purpose is, seem to struggle the most with a lack of energy. Without that understanding, the drive to move onward and upward is not there.

The same can be seen in classrooms everywhere. When the purpose is not clear to students, they are not engaged. When students are not engaged, behavior issues tend to creep in and test scores are subpar. I know from experience the reality of this.

I will never forget the time I was dragged (and I am not exaggerating here) to the principal's office. I was in fifth grade. I remember it like it was yesterday....

"Class… take out your textbooks and go to page 242." My stomach churned. I *hated* reading. We were supposed to have read the chapter already in preparation for a discussion of the material. As always, I hadn't. I remember the students actively discussing the details with the teacher. I went into my usual slump. I decided to pull out my new bendy pencil I had bought the day before with the change I had found on the floor by my dad's side of the bed. I whipped it around and it accidently struck the textbook, leaving a mark. Quickly, I glanced around to see if anyone saw what I had done. My eyes landed on a boy named Ramon.

Oh no! He saw!

But Ramon did something I did not expect. He smiled and seemed to be entertained by my cool bendy pencil and its ability to whip and leave stray marks.

Ahhhh, an audience! I have a new purpose! Clearly Ramon was just as bored as I was!

Never fear, Ramon, Jennifer is here! I will save us both from the dullness that surrounds us!

Then, with all the gusto my bendy pencil and I could muster, I whipped that textbook page into submission!

Take that! And That! AND THAT!

I had saved the day! Ramon was giggling! It was a glorious moment to behold! Until…. a gasp was heard nearby... a boy named Damian shot his hand into the air as if it were some sort of emergency flare!

"Teacher, Jennifer wrote all over her book!" he declared.

The cold sweat of reality swept over my entire body. Before I knew what was happening, my teacher was next to my desk, grabbing my arm.

The alarm bells were sounding off in my head as she pulled me up and began to march me to the door. Laughter erupted behind me. We continued moving forward, marching down the hall.

"Where are we going?" I finally found the voice to ask.

"To the office!" her booming voice declared.

NOOOOOOO! Not the office! They torture kids there!

I had heard the stories. Like the time someone had to hold a stack of encyclopedias for an hour. Not to mention the paddle... I will never forget the time in first grade when the assistant principal, a six foot something, Harley riding man with more facial hair than Santa Claus, came to show me the paddle he had and would use, if I didn't behave. The image of the holes and worn looking handle is still seared into my brain. How many times did he use that thing to get such a patina?

Once again, reality swept over me. "Please, please, don't take me!" I screamed. "I'm sorry! I'll erase it! I'm sorry!"

"I'm sick of it!" she shouted back.

Sick of what? I had never done this before.

25

Just then, we rounded the corner. The office was just steps away. A feeling of defeat overcame me.

She's not going to change her mind. She's not going to turn around.

Immediately, my arms and butt began to ache in anticipation… We walked inside the dreaded door. She steered me to a chair and discarded me into it. She went over and whispered to the secretary, but her flailing arms and pointing fingers told me everything I needed to know. This was the big time, the main event. I was busted.

Sitting there, while waiting for my sentencing, I remembered something I had brought with me to school that day. Carefully, I pulled out a little card I had gotten at church the Sunday before. It had been contoured by my pocket, edges bent. On one side was a picture of Jesus, the other had reminders of the person we need to strive to be. I took one look at it and began to bawl.

You are not a good person, Jen.

The principal, in her great wisdom, gave me time to sit and deliver my own punishment. I have no doubt the secretary went into her office to inform her of the situation and how I was carrying on.

Finally, the secretary told me to go in. I wiped my tear streaked face and I could feel the heat pulsing around my now puffy eye-lids. My legs felt like lead and my heart pounded in my chest. Cautiously, I entered…

She sat behind her desk, wisdom wrinkles adorning her face, a crocheted shawl around her shoulders like a super hero's cape. She emitted something I had not expected, love... unconditional love and understanding. It took me off-guard. Where was the stack of encyclopedias?

Then, I saw her lips part, "Why did you do that to your book?" she questioned.

No yelling. Just a calm question.

"I... I was bored," I stammered.

She peered over her glasses and asked, "Will you do that again?"

"No," I said as I glanced around the room still looking for evidence of the torture devices I had been lead to believe were there.

"Well, okay then." She looked back down to the papers fanned across her desk.

I stood there, numb.

Okay then, what?

She looked back up with an expression of surprise to still see me standing there.

"You may go now," she assured.

Hesitantly, I turned to go. I didn't know what to say. No punishment? No yelling? No phone call to my mom?

Reality of being released hit and I quickly left in fear of her changing her mind. I remember walking back, confused, but grateful, and I had a new respect and reverence for my principal that I will never forget.

Looking back on this experience I hold no negative feelings toward the teacher that took me to the office or guilt associated with what I had done. Honestly I can say I am so grateful it happened. More than anything it taught me the importance of being sure students understand purpose.

My right-brain dominance can be such a positive influence when it comes to understanding the big picture, but it can be my detriment, too. If I do not understand the "why?" behind what is being done or is being asked of me, I shut down. So often classrooms are just moving forward without even a mention of the purpose for what is happening. There is no connection to the big picture.

If you were to come to my classroom, you would see the large and colorful "WHY?" I have permanently put in the middle of my white board. It serves a dual purpose. First, it provides a launching point when I introduce a new skill or topic. Second, it is also a reminder for students to support their ideas by including the "why" in their answers.

By discussing with them why we are doing what we are doing, purpose is established. To take this concept a step further, I also tie in how what we are learning also corresponds with who they want to be. This leads me back to the beginning of this chapter. Many of us teachers talk with the kids about who they want to be and may do an activity related to this, but do not use it as a tool. Let me share with you one way you can.

As in the chapter before, I would encourage you to use these tools for yourself. By doing so, you will benefit from them and be more prepared to share them with your students.

First, begin by making a list of what you are good at. There is no limit, but I have drawn a few handy little lines for you to use.

_____

_____

_____

_____

_____

_____

_____

_____

_____

_____

_____

_____

The reason for doing this is to recognize and celebrate your current skills, talents, and abilities. This also helps get the brain prepared for the next step.

Second, think about the person you want to become. What skills, attributes, profession you would like that you do not already have? Write them down:

_____

_____

_____

_____

_____

_____

_____

_____

_____

_____

Congratulations, you have now set your purpose! Knowing who you are and who you want to become is the fuel to drive you to be the person you were born to be. In my classroom, after the students have made their lists, we convert them into visual candy. I give them each an empty outline like the one below and they draw pictures inside the outline to go with each word. They illustrate both what they are good at and who they want to become. Physical features are not included (like eyes, teeth, etc.) My students and I refer to this as our Purpose Person.

This is available to download from our website:
www.classroomelements.com

I would encourage you to make your own Purpose Person, too. I made one, but I used clip-art and magazine pictures to illustrate mine. It is hanging in a spot I see and refer to daily. Now when I say refer to, I do not just mean glance at. I like to spend time with my person. I acknowledge and celebrate which illustrations I am and I "play" with what I want to become. I do this by imagining with my 5 senses (see, smell, hear, taste, feel).

I also taught my students to do this as well. It is a great way to interact with your person and remind yourself of who you want to be. I taught my students when they are looking at their person to imagine how it will look when they gain that skill/ attribute or become who they want to. What will they hear? How will they feel? It is fun to discuss with them how it will taste, too. My class and I laughed ourselves silly when we were doing this together as a class. One student wants to become a Marine so when we got to taste he declared, "I don't know how I will taste, but maybe sweaty and salty because I will be moving a lot!"

Smell may even be a part of that "visualization" too. On my Purpose Person, I have a picture of a woman eating a strawberry. Under the picture I wrote, "a raw and organic eater". So I imagine the smell of fresh, healthy food coming to my mouth. Use whatever sense is appropriate to aid in imagining your desired result.

Once all the students had their Purpose Person complete, they shared it with their team (the group they sit with during the day). Throughout the year, their Purpose People are constantly used. Each morning they refer to their person to remind themselves of the person they are and want to become. Whenever I introduce a new skill, we discuss how that skill will help the students in their journey to becoming who they want to be.

For example, we were beginning our measurement unit and I gave an overview of the skills we would be learning. I asked students to challenge me to see if I could prove what we were learning in measurement had to do with who they want to become as far as their future jobs go. The students thought it was so cool how everyone needed to know about the skills that we were going to learn. For one student the excitement spilled out as she declared, "You really proved it good, Ms. Coon. We all need to learn this!"

Some of you may ask, "Is it really worth the time?" The short answer to this is, "YES!" But, some of us require a bit more than that. Let me just remind you of yourself. How many times have you been asked or told to do something for which you could not understand the purpose? You probably did it anyway, but how did you feel? Connected? Engaged? Or, did you just go through the motions?

Bottom line is this, I expect my students to explain the reason "why" during discussions and to demonstrate their understanding. With this being said, why wouldn't I hold that same expectation for myself? If one chooses to hold the "because I told you so" near and dear to their heart, students will be lost and disconnections will be solidified. Please don't let this happen. I would hate for someone else to have to resort to using their bendy pencil, too. Find your purpose and lead your students to do the same! You will see immediate results.

Tool in a nutshell: Who I Am

Why? What is the purpose? To identify strengths and desired characteristics which will lead humans to their purpose and propel them forward.

- Begin by writing down a list of what you are good at.
- Next write down traits, skills, abilities, etc. you want to possess/ who you want to become.
- Create a visual representation of who you are and would like to become.
- Refer to your representation often, at least daily.
- My students keep theirs in their data binders along with their test scores and declaration.
- Visualize the person you are striving to become or wish to continue to be:
  - How will it/ you look?
  - How will it/ you feel?
  - What will you hear?
  - How will it taste?
  - How will it smell?

Variations: Who I Am

- When working with less than enthusiastic individuals (like middle school and high school students), the lists alone are a good start. These can still be referred to in establishing purpose. Images are more powerful, but not absolutely necessary.
- One of the adults I mentor drew an outline of herself and wrote sentences describing who she is and wants to be. She reads it each day like a declaration.

Let's do some reflecting now. Use the t-chart to write down how exploring who one is and wants to become can improve your life How can you use this information to improve another's life?

Your Life	Another's Life

5
MAKE IT HAPPEN:
VISION BOARDS

Just a few years ago, I thought I had no time. School and home responsibilities seemed to consume my every minute. I had bought into the thinking "I am doing the best I can." I have since realized that I was allowing school and home responsibilities to consume my *thoughts* and by doing so, my time was being spent in very unproductive ways. In essence, it felt like I had no time because I spent my energy dwelling on things I needed to do, wanted to do, or things that were just plain out of my control.

Over the last year, I have received two grants for my school. I was nominated and became the second runner-up for teacher of the year in my school district. I organized and hosted the first family reunion for my family. I wrote this book. I started Classroom Elements and trained educational personnel at the elementary, middle, and high school levels. I mentored adults and children. I started raising my own chickens. I also taught another year of second grade, participated in the after-school program, and gardened at school and at home. In addition, I began training for another half marathon, improved my home, and took care of my family.

Now the above is not a list I use to brag and boast. It is a list of some of my accomplishments. It is evidence to myself that I am moving forward and am not stagnant. I share this with you to show you how, just by changing my frame of mind, I could take on more. Now I am living life and loving it! I am not allowing life to just happen to me.

I use this next tool to help me achieve things I would have never imagined before. Each one of those accomplishments started with writing down what I wanted or by getting a picture of what I wanted and taping it in a designated area next to my bed. I look at it both morning and night and "play" with it by visualizing, like I do my Purpose Person. The tool I am referring to is a vision board.

So, what is a vision board? Why do I use it, and encourage others to do the same? Basically, the vision board provides direction and focus to help you to achieve your purpose and become the person you want to be. In chapter 4, I shared with you how vital it is to find one's purpose. Vision boards are a great way to help you set goals to move you toward that purpose.

For example, on my Purpose Person I have a picture of a woman riding a bike and under the picture I wrote, "Physically Active." Being a physically active person is who I want to be. But for me, knowing that and visualizing is not enough. I must set goals to help me achieve who I want to be. I am presently training to be in another half marathon. On my vision board, I have put my registration for the El Paso Marathon. Every morning and night I visualize my participation during the half marathon using all of my senses. By doing this, I no longer need to force myself and spend lots of mental energy to be physically active. My subconscious knows what I need to do and I go into auto-pilot to make it become a reality.

The really cool part is when I complete that half marathon, I will be excited to take my registration slip off my vision board and place it into my achievements binder. I love my achievements binder! It serves as a wonderful reminder for myself of what can be accomplished after I put something on my vision board.

I also use vision boards in my classroom. Each student has their own. They are encouraged to put things they want to achieve both personally and academically on their own boards. Preparation for mandated tests becomes intrinsic as students set their goals for their desired outcome. It is awesome to look at their vision boards and see things like:

I want to get an 80 or better on my big test.
(She included a hand-drawn picture of a rectangle with a 80 on it to aid in visualization.)

I want to learn 5 words in French.
(With a picture of a stick figure with words in a speech bubble.)

I want to have all green days this week.
(In correlation to the behavior system I use in class.)

I love to watch the excitement in their eyes as they remove something from their vision boards and put it in the achieved section of their notebooks. It is so amazing to see how second graders know what they need to work on, set their own goals, review their goals, and monitor their progress toward achievement or attainment.

Since I began using vision boards in my classroom, I have seen improved test scores and focus. For example, one of the mandated tests our school district uses to monitor progress is done on the computer. It tests their abilities in math and reading. Once they have completed their test, I am able to print out a computer generated report that has a line graph that indicates performance increase, decrease, or stagnancy in comparison to the previous test.

The student's score is indicated with a blue line. After the initial beginning of the year test, students set goals like "I want to have my blue line go up in math." To aid in visualization, they even added a blue line with a crayon, slanting in an upward direction.

I would frequently hear someone during group work say, "Okay guys, we really need to work hard on this because I want my blue line to go up." The purpose was set, the desire was there, and I was allowed to be a facilitator in helping them achieve those desired outcomes.

On a personal level, I use my vision board to post both things I want to achieve and things I wish to attain. Take, for instance, the time I realized the need to secure an office space for Classroom Elements. I knew I did not want to spend a lot of money or get anything like a small business loan. Classroom Elements is a volunteer based organization. Now the "old" Jen would have stewed and stewed over the situation and turned it into a dilemma, but not anymore. Instead, I placed that desire on my vision board. Doing this was the hardest part because I knew this was a big step. It meant our organization was moving to the next level. Those nasty nervous butterflies snuck their way in and when that happened, I knew I was on the right track! This was going to be another way to challenge myself. After I thanked the butterflies for visiting, I let go of all worry and concern. I did not stew about it. I knew a solution would present itself.

That night, before bed, I visualized the space I wanted to attain for us. I knew we needed a private room for mentoring appointments, but we also needed a large space for group meetings. I imagined a place with good energy, just enough space, quiet, and no funky smells. Then, I drifted off to sleep.

Three o'clock a.m. came and I was awakened with a solution! I got my laptop and went to Craig's List. Now, I must tell you that I had never been on Craig's List before. I had heard of it, but never investigated it myself. Now there I was, before the birds had even begun to stir, navigating my way around the unfamiliar site. I came across a listing that looked promising. I emailed the contact and by that afternoon found myself at the perfect location for our office. It had everything we needed!

This is just one example, but vision boards have proven to be powerful time and time again. By posting what it is that you want to achieve or attain, you can let it go from your mind. Revisit it every morning and night, but don't dwell on it. I have found that dwelling does nothing more than waste energy and cloud our minds. When we free our minds, we open ourselves to inspiration.

An Important Lesson:

One day, while making my daily vision board rounds in my classroom, I saw a new sticky note on one of my student's boards that brought tears to my eyes. It said, "I want my mom and dad to live together again." It had a little picture of two stick figures holding hands with a heart floating above them. He had seen the power of the vision board in accomplishing and attaining his goals and desires. But I had to remind him that what we put on our vision board must not involve others choices in order to become a reality. Essentially, what one wants cannot be solely dependent on the choices of others.

Much like when I was working on filling out the teacher of the year application. I had been nominated and now I was facing my arch nemesis, paperwork. I knew I wanted to put something on my vision board about the whole teacher of the year process, but I struggled with what to put. Some of my friends suggested I put "I want to be teacher of the year" on my vision board, but it did not sit right with me. I knew the ultimate decision was up to a committee. It depended on their choices.

Finally, I decided to put on my vision board that I would complete and turn in my application. This was still something that made me uneasy. In fact, about five years earlier I had been nominated and decided to not even bother returning the paper work because it all seemed like too much. This time I welcomed that uneasy feeling knowing that if I could push past the yucky feelings, I would grow as a person. Now that the experience is over, I can look back and see I did grow.

Making a vision board is simple and there are many ways to do it. The bottom line is that you need a defined area that is not too big or too small. I will share with you the three different types of vision boards I am actively involved with. The one near my bed was made by just cutting 4 pieces of ribbon (about 18 inches each) and forming a square. I attached the ribbon onto the wall by using ticky-tack. Those things I wish to obtain are secured to the wall with ticky-tack, too.

The vision board we have at Classroom Elements is a 2' X 2' board with ribbons crisscrossing it. My team and I write on index cards and slip them under the ribbons indicating what we want.

My students' vision boards are pieces of card stock that were hung on the wall with an index card over each one identifying whose was whose. Students write down what they want on sticky notes that can be removed easily once it is achieved. I had started out by having their vision boards in their data binders, but decided to move them to the wall for all to see.

This leads me to an important aspect of vision boards. Do not hide your vision boards! Others can help you attain what you desire, too! Now there is a BIG difference between relying on other's choices to attain or achieve something, versus receiving from someone to help you attain or achieve your goals.

It is incredible to watch this happen in my classroom. They are aware of what is on each other's vision boards, and the dialogue in the classroom reflects that. My students have assigned partners. One day I heard one of them tell their partner, "I saw you want to get a 100 on your spelling test. Do you want to practice with me after we finish breakfast?" Now y'all, how cool is that!?!

So, to wrap it up, vision boards are wonderful instruments that will lead you toward your purpose or even continue your purpose. Also, one of the best things you can put on your vision board is something that is making you get a severe attack of those nasty butterflies. Those are the aspirations, that when accomplished or attained, will move you in an upward direction. You will grow as a person!

So long, survival mode... Hello, soaring mode!

Tool in a nutshell: Vision Boards

Why? What is the purpose? To set butterfly inducing goals to help you achieve your purpose.

- Begin by finding a place to put your vision board. Remember, don't hide it!
- It can take any form you wish, but don't waste too much time making the perfect one. A piece of card stock, a border made with ribbon or tape, or a cork board will even do. I have even seen software online to make one.
- Pick something you wish to attain or accomplish, preferably something that invites the butterflies over to play.
- Write what you want down on a paper or find an image to represent what it is.
- Post it on your vision board.
- Repeat, if desired, but don't go overboard... like under 10! Keep it real.
- Morning and Night visualize what it is you want:
  - How will it/ you look?
  - How will it/ you feel?
  - What will you hear?

- o How will it taste?
- o How will it smell?
- Aim to keep your mind "open" to receive inspiration to accomplish your goals.

Variations: **Vision Boards**

- In middle and high school classrooms, I have heard of students using sticky notes in their notebook for their goals quite effectively. It is just important to have them dedicate one place for current goals, and another for them to move their sticky notes to after they have achieved them.
- Dedicating a time for sharing achievements with others (like in a classroom or meeting) is a wonderful extension, too.

Let's do some reflecting now. Use the t-chart to write down how using a vision board can improve your life. How you can use this information to improve another's life?

Your Life	Another's Life

6
WHEN THOSE YUCKIES FILL YOU UP:
JOURNALING

I remember the day starting like most days. The kids came into the classroom, began their morning routine without a hitch, ate breakfast, read declarations, visualized at their vision boards, reminded themselves of the person they wanted to be. It was now 8:15 and like most days, Susanna's (name changed for obvious reasons) chair still remained empty. I hoped all was well and continued with the day.

Fifteen minutes later, I was in full swing, teaching something fascinating about reading, when the door slowly opened. I glanced over and immediately knew Susanna's day started off in the wrong direction. Her head hung low, tear tracks streaked her cheeks, and I could see her lip quivering from across the room. Now the "old" Jen would have stopped the lesson, barked out a quick assignment/activity to give the class something to do while I met with Susanna. This time, I didn't. I just kept teaching. She walked up to me, handed me her tardy slip, and our eyes met.

"Are you okay," I asked.

All she could do was nod.

"Did you get your feelings hurt?" I questioned.

"My sister said something mean to me and I let the yuckies get in me," she responded.

"Do you remember what to do?" I asked.

She nodded.

"Okay, I will check on you in a little bit. Go take care of those yuckies," I said.

Off she went. The lesson continued without hardly missing a beat.

She hung up her backpack and then immediately reached for her data binder. Next, she took out one of her journals and began to write. I knew she was headed in the right direction, so my focus returned to the remainder of the class. Our lesson continued and before I knew it, Susanna was laughing and smiling with her peers as her group participated in a discussion with one another. Joy instantly filled me as quickly as it seemed to fill her.

She must have felt my gaze because in a matter of seconds she looked over to me. I gave her a thumbs up and a huge smile. She returned the expression. All was well in our corner of the planet again.

There is a wonderful book called *Andrew's Angry Words*, by Dorothea Lachner that I read to my students. It illustrates what happened to Susanna beautifully. Essentially, the story is about a young boy, named

Andrew, who gets upset at his sister and yells angry words at her. Then, the story shows a negative reaction as a ball of angry words gets passed from person to person. Finally, a wise woman gathers the ball of yucky negativity and throws it into the ocean, thereby discontinuing the negative chain reaction that was taking place.

This sort of negative chain reaction happens all the time on our planet. People's emotional cups can easily and sometimes instantly be filled up. Those cups can be especially dangerous when filled with negativity. In the story, Andrew's cup became full of angry emotion and it spilled all over his sister causing her to become angry. In the case of my student, Susanna, her sister said something hurtful to her causing Susanna's cup to fill up with negativity. In fact, her cup was so full of negativity, she began to cry. BUT, Susanna held onto the negativity just long enough to get it out of her in a "safe" way.

Thanks to Susanna's willingness to learn what to do when she finds she has a full cup of negative emotion and it is about to spill over, the ball of negativity did not get passed to anyone else. She took out her "yucky" journal that we had made using two pieces of black construction paper and some filler paper, and she wrote out all the negative feelings she had inside her. It was a safe place to dump it. Nobody else got hurt and Susanna was able to empty her cup of negativity. In my classroom, nobody else, not even me, reads other's yucky journals. Goodness knows, there may be something in there about me! Do I want to fill up my cup and make it spill over? No way!

In addition to a yucky journal, the students in my class have a yummy journal. I learned from one of my mentors that after releasing negativity, it is important to think of positive things. I found out later from Susanna that she remembered to do this, too. Immediately after dumping out her yuckies, she pulled out her yummy journal and wrote down something that had made her laugh the night before.

Teaching students to journal with a purpose is so important. First, it gives them a safe outlet. Second, it teaches them that they can manage their emotions. I am not sure why it is, but it seems common place to look to others to solve our problems and make us feel better. What happens when there is nobody there to help? Journaling is a powerful way to manage and analyze our own emotions.

If someone would have told me five years ago that I would be saying today that journaling is one of the most POWERFUL tools on the planet, I would have laughed my head off! Well... it is! I used to think of journaling as something one would do as a record of their life for future generations to read and enjoy. I really did not buy into that purpose. Now, I view it as a way to get out negativity and to look for trends or cycles of negativity that seem to visit my mind frequently. I use it to write letters to people that I never intend to mail when there are things I need to say to them without dumping on them. On the positive side, I use journaling to write down my "ah-ha" moments and happy memories.

I have my own set of yummy and yucky journals. The students see me use mine from time to time, too. I celebrate the idea of leading by example, but most importantly, I use them for me and the "safety" of others.

Gone are my days of dumping or venting. Most times, when I struggle with the urge to vent, I am not seeking an audience. I am not looking for advice. I just need to get it out. Rather than dumping my emotional trash on someone- I PUT IT DOWN ON PAPER!

One of my dear friends is a venter, but it is something she is working hard to overcome. A few months ago, she was very concerned about something and felt as though she had been wronged. She vented to several people, including myself. I was quiet and listened, but I did not let it affect me. Another friend was not as lucky, she later shared with me that after taking the emotional garbage that was dumped on her, she was left feeling like she had been slapped in the face. Sad part is, it had nothing at all to do with her.

Please, don't be like Andrew! Don't pass on negativity!

Bonus Material:

There is another really cool part about writing things down that helps you take on more. How many of you feel like you are in a constant state of chaos? Would you like to know a probable reason? You are hanging onto too much in your consciousness! Use the power of the pen and paper to get it out so you can let it go!

Nearly all of the educational personnel I mentored at the end of the school year felt as though they were in a state of chaos. They were trying to remember it all! Their mind was cluttered! By taking just a few minutes to write down things you need to do or are concerned you may forget, you will free your mind! A free mind is open to insight and inspiration.

At Classroom Elements, one of our favorite things we like to pass out to others is a simple 3" X 5" Memo Book. My dad used these when I was growing up. He called them his brain books. A principal I gave one to told me that before she goes to bed, she writes down everything that is on her mind. She explained that by doing this, she is letting it go and placing it in the hands of her higher power.

Now, some of you may be thinking, "Why not just put it in my smart phone?" Great idea! If that works for you, do it! Personally, it did not work for me. It was too much for my A.D.D. and took too long to put things in. For me, paper and pen is much faster, but use something! Don't try to manage it all in your mind because it might just cause your cup to spill over!

Tool in a nutshell: Journaling

Why? What is the purpose? To manage negativity on an ongoing basis and to stay focused on the positive. To keep the mind clear and free.

- Designate two journals, one for good and yummy thoughts and the other for negative and yucky thoughts.

- Use accordingly, but remember after dumping out negative emotions, write down good thoughts and feelings.

- Don't hold onto things in your consciousness, WRITE IT DOWN, don't pass it on or allow it to create a sense of chaos in your mind.

- My students are encouraged to write in their journals first thing in the morning and are encouraged to do so as needed throughout the day.

Variations: Journaling

- One of my mentors from when I first started teaching came to one of my trainings where I shared the power of journaling. I asked her for her feedback and she shared with me how it might be good to call the journals by something other than yucky and yummy so, as students get older, it will not be an issue. I am so grateful for her input. Feel free to call them whatever suits you and/or students. Upper grade classes can use positive and negative, etc. For me, I personally like yucky and yummy and I am an adult (although sometimes deep-down, I still feel like I'm eight).

Let's do some reflecting now. Use the t-chart below to write down how journaling can improve your life and how using them can improve another's life.

Your Life	Another's Life

7
BOOM, BOOM, LA-LA-LA!:
MUSIC

If you were to come to Loma Heights Elementary at 7:50 a.m., you would see our staff and students lined up with their classes out on the back blacktop. Many would be moving to the beat of a song like Katy Perry's *Firework*. Some students would even be belting out the lyrics.

Each morning, as I make the forty minute journey from the great state of Texas to New Mexico, the land of enchantment, I prepare for the day with songs like Heather Small's *Proud*.

One cannot deny the power of music, the messages, and the emotion. Yet, how often do we harness that power? It is so common. We can easily take it for granted. It is time to start viewing music in our personal lives and classrooms as a tool that can take our lives to the next level.

I believe the more we can pump positive messages into ourselves, the better. Music is a powerful way to do this. I have felt a change in my personal life and a shift in the classroom, when positive music is used.

During the past school year, my niece, Vanessa, introduced me to a song that quickly became a favorite with my students. It is called *What I Am* by Will.i.Am. It is a song that was featured on Sesame Street and I was able to access it on You Tube. My students began referring to it as *The Truth Song* and I found it a very effective tool in quickly lifting class morale.

Later, one of my students introduced us to the song Don't Give Up by Bruno Mars that he found on You Tube. We often sang it, too, as it always brought about a positive energy shift in the classroom.

When my students enter the classroom in the morning, I like to have a song with a positive beat and a positive message playing. Positive beat? Yes, something with the beat found in dance/pop music. Dance breaks and dance parties are common place in my class, too. It is a great reward for the class that does not cost any money. It is during those dance breaks, interesting observations can be made. Insecurity may rear it's nasty head, but I find that by getting out there and dancing myself without drawing any attention to their lack of participation, they eventually come around and move, too.

So get your groove on and find those songs that are out there with messages you want to have repeating in your head! Learn the lyrics and sing at the top of your lungs! You will not regret it!

Tool in a nutshell: Music

Why? What is the purpose? To pump positive and uplifting messages into the mind.

- Locate music with a positive message.
- Learn the lyrics.
- Play it often, but the beginning of the day is especially effective in setting your mood in a positive direction.
- To take it up a notch, dance!

Let's do some reflecting now. Use the t-chart below to record how using positive music can improve your life and another's life.

Your Life	Another's Life

8
CONCLUDING NUGGETS

Hi! If this is the first page of the book you are reading, welcome! Yes, I know about you people who read the end first to see if a book is any good. I hope those of you who started at the beginning will agree with me that this is a good book. Let us continue...

At the beginning of the school year, I asked my students what they do when they feel sad, angry, or are feeling bad about themselves. Most of them could not give an answer. Some said they would cry. By the end of the year, they all could tell me exactly what tools they could use. I compiled a list of *their ideas* I would like to share with you.

- Write the yuckies in your journal!
- Say the truth (declaration).
- Stop them in your brain.
- Think of good things and write them down.
- Forget and forgive!

Through daily cultivation, my students left the classroom with a firm foundation in using tools for the next time those yucky, negative feelings come their way.

Additionally, at the beginning of the school year, when asked why they were coming to school, I received very vague and general answers such as "because it is important" or "so I can read better", etc. By the end of the year, they could give me specific reasons they come to school and how it helps them prepare for who they want to become.

I have shared with you tools that are not new to the planet that I have learned about and incorporated into my life and my classroom. I no longer struggle with negative messages like I used to, and I have taught adults and students to do the same. I have found my purpose and encourage my students and others to do the same. With this being said, using these tools is not a quick fix or a fad diet. It takes time, repetition, and effort. This is not a Band-Aid or magic fairy dust, but these tools will prepare you and your students' hearts for learning and inspiration. It is well worth the effort!

These tools can be used in conjunction with all sorts of things! I also use what I have learned from Steven Covey in *The Leader in Me* and *7 Habits for Happy Kids* by Sean Covey in conjunction with what I have shared with you in this book. I think they go together like cottage cheese and pineapple, with a dash of pepper.

No matter what you choose to do with the information I have shared with you, please remember this… there are a tremendous number of humans roaming this planet without purpose. They are succumbing to negativity. Don't become, or continue to be, one of them. It is never too late to change! **This planet needs warriors of light and beacons of positivity for the next generation.** Begin to SOAR today!

ABOUT THE AUTHOR

Jennifer Coon (jen@classroomelements.com) was born and raised in El Paso, Texas. She graduated with honors from New Mexico State University in 2002 with a bachelor's degree in Elementary Education. She is a teacher in the Las Cruces Public Schools district in Las Cruces, New Mexico. She has taught first grade for five years and second grade for five years at Loma Heights Elementary. She currently lives in El Paso, Texas and is an avid gardener and D.I.Y.er. She mentors and trains educational personnel in conjunction with Classroom Elements (www.classroomelements.com).